Think About It

Beverly Courrege

A JANET THOMA BOOK

THOMAS NELSON PUBLISHERS
Nashville

Published in Nashville, Tennessee, by Thomas Nelson, Inc., Publishers.
The Bible version used in this publication is THE NEW KING JAMES VERSION. Copyright © 1979, 1980, 1982, 1990, Thomas Nelson, Inc., Publishers.

Library of Congress Cataloging-in-Publication Data

Courrege, Beverly.
    WWJD? : think about it / Beverly Courrege.
        p.   cm.
    ISBN 0-7852-8212-2
    1. Jesus Christ—Example. 2. Jesus Christ—Influence. 3. Christian life. I. Title.
BT304.2.C68   1998
248.4—dc21   98-7202
CIP

Printed in the United States of America.

1 2 3 4 5 6 QPK 03 02 01 00 99 98

*This book is dedicated to all those who
"walk with Jesus daily" in the ability that God supplies,
that in all things God may be glorified through
Jesus Christ to whom the glory belongs.*

CONTENTS

Acknowledgments

Special acknowledgment to Charles Sheldon who introduced the timeless concept of "What Would Jesus Do" through his ministry and writing more than one hundred years ago.

I thank God always for the many friends and family members who have encouraged me in all that I do, especially in writing!

Thanks to Boo, my number one encourager, whose life reflects the example of "What Would Jesus Do?" in all that he does.

And to Cord and Jennifer, I thank God that in His plan for me he allowed me to be your mother. I love you.

INTRODUCTION

WWJD? Giving Credit Where Credit Is Due

Despite all the enthusiasm in the past few years, WWJD is not about a cool logo on T-shirts, caps, and some 15 million bracelets around the world. It is about a radical change in thinking and living. Only one Person can effect that kind of change; therefore, the credit for WWJD goes to our Lord. What would Jesus say in response to this phenomenon? "Be doers of the word, and not hearers only" (James 1:22).

So, in light of that challenge, *WWJD? Think About It* presents you with several ways to zero in on being a doer. First, each of the book's seven sections begins with an excerpt from *In His Steps* by Charles Sheldon. This classic novel was written in the 1890s. Sheldon, a young minister in Topeka, Kansas, went around the city disguised as an unemployed printer. Burdened by the lack of compassion he found in the Christian community, he began writing submissions to a newspaper. These articles later were incorporated into a book, which sold 2 million copies upon its release.

The final chapter of *In His Steps* shows the impact the book has made on our culture and hints at a prophetic vision Sheldon had. In the last chapter the fictional pastor has a vision in which he sees banners with the words WHAT WOULD JESUS DO? at some great convention.

Fast forward one hundred years. At the 1997–98 Christian Bookseller's Association Convention in Atlanta, Georgia, the acronym WWJD? was visible on banners from one side of the convention floor to the other. Naysayers call it a fad, but hardly so after a century.

Second, each section of the book contains questions concerning situations you face in everyday life, leading up to the WWJD question. Finally, in each section there are verses from God's Word, which establish how we are to respond. Some of the Scriptures answer "What would Jesus do?" because Jesus Himself faced these situations. Some of the Scriptures, however, answer the questions that we, imperfect as we are, face in this imperfect world—more of a "What would Jesus have us do?" approach. Either way, God's Word is clear . . . and timeless.

Use *WWJD? Think About It* as a road map, a jump start, or maybe as a challenge to step up and become a student of the rest of God's Word . . . and become what He truly intends you to be.

PART I

What Does It Mean, "Follow Me"?

A stranger walks off the street interrupting Rev. Henry Maxwell's Sunday morning sermon to the First Church of Raymond:

"I'm not an ordinary tramp, though I don't know of any teaching of Jesus that makes one kind of a tramp less worth saving than another. Do you?" He put the question as naturally as if the whole congregation had been a small Bible class. He paused just a moment and coughed painfully. Then he went on.

"I lost my job ten months ago. I am a printer by trade . . ."

After describing his situation he continues.

W

W

J

D

?

"There are a good many others like me. I'm not complaining, am I? Just stating the facts. But I was wondering as I sat there under the gallery, if what you call following Jesus is the same thing as what He taught. What did He mean when He said: 'Follow me!' The minister said," here the man turned about and looked up at the pulpit, "that it is necessary for the disciple of Jesus to follow His steps, and he said the steps are 'obedience, faith, love and imitation.' But I did not hear him tell you just what he meant that to mean, especially the last step. What do you Christians mean by following the steps of Jesus?"

—from Chapter One of *In His Steps* by Charles Sheldon

3

Have you ever been unjustly angry?

WWJD?

But now you yourselves are to put off all these: anger, wrath, malice, blasphemy, filthy language out of your mouth. (Col. 3:8)

Have you ever been judgmental?

WWJD?

Therefore you are inexcusable, O man, whoever you are who judge, for in whatever you judge another you condemn yourself; for you who judge practice the same things. (Rom. 2:1)

4

W

W

J

D

?

Have you ever had a waitress who just couldn't get it right?

WWJD?

By your patience possess your souls. (Luke 21:19)

Have you ever offended anyone by smoking in a crowded area?

WWJD?

All things are lawful for me, but not all things are helpful; all things are lawful for me, but not all things edify. Let no one seek his own, but each one the other's well-being. (1 Cor. 10:23–24)

5

Have you ever been ashamed?

WWJD?

Not by works of righteousness which we have done, but according to His mercy He saved us, through the washing of regeneration and renewing of the Holy Spirit. (Titus 3:5)

Have you ever been known by your good example to others?

WWJD?

For I rejoiced greatly when brethren came and testified of the truth that is in you, just as you walk in the truth. (3 John 3)

6

W

W

J

D

?

Have you ever chosen not to study the Bible?

WWJD?

For the word of God is living and powerful, and sharper than any two-edged sword, piercing even to the division of soul and spirit, and of joints and marrow, and is a discerner of the thoughts and intents of the heart. And there is no creature hidden from His sight, but all things are naked and open to the eyes of Him to whom we must give account. (Heb. 4:12–13)

7

Have you ever fallen short?

WWJD?

For all have sinned and fall short of the glory of God, being justified freely by His grace through the redemption that is in Christ Jesus. (Rom. 3:23–24)

But God demonstrates His own love toward us, in that while we were still sinners, Christ died for us. (Rom. 5:8)

W

W

J

D

?

Have you ever been ridiculed for your faith?

WWJD?

Beloved, do not think it strange concerning the fiery trial which is to try you, as though some strange thing happened to you; but rejoice to the extent that you partake of Christ's sufferings, that when His glory is revealed, you may also be glad with exceeding joy. (1 Peter 4:12–13)

Have you ever lost a loved one?

WWJD?

But I do not want you to be ignorant, brethren, concerning those who have fallen asleep, lest you sorrow as others who have no hope. For if we believe that Jesus died and rose again, even so God will bring with Him those who sleep in Jesus. (1 Thess. 4:13–14)

W

W

J

D

?

10

Have you ever been tempted?

WWJD?

Again, the devil took Him up on an exceedingly high mountain, and showed Him all the kingdoms of the world and their glory. And he said to Him, "All these things I will give You if You will fall down and worship me." Then Jesus said to him, "Away with you, Satan!" (Matt. 4:8–10a)

PART 2

Any Volunteers?

One week after the stranger spoke to the First Church, Rev. Maxwell challenges himself and his congregation with these words:

"The appearance and words of this stranger in the church last Sunday made a powerful impression on me. I am not able to conceal from you or myself the fact that what he said, followed as it has been by his death in my house, has compelled me to ask as I never asked before 'What does following Jesus mean?' I am not in a position yet to utter any condemnation of this people or, to a certain extent, to myself, either in our Christ-like relations to this man or the numbers that he represents in the world. But all that does not prevent me from feeling that much that the man said was so vitally true that we must face it in

an attempt to answer it or else stand condemned as
Christian disciples."

*Rev. Maxwell looked into the faces of his people and closed his
sermon with the following proposal:*

"I want volunteers from the First Church who will
pledge themselves, earnestly and honestly for an entire
year, not to do anything without first asking the question,
'What would Jesus do?' And after asking that question,
each one will follow Jesus exactly as he knows how, no
matter what the result may be. I will of course include
myself in this company of volunteers, and shall take for
granted that my church here will not be surprised at my
future conduct, as based upon this standard of action, and

will not oppose whatever is done if they think Christ would do it."

— from Chapter Two of *In His Steps* by Charles Sheldon

W

W

J

D

?

Have you ever felt helpless?

WWJD?

I can do all things through Christ who strengthens me.
(Phil. 4:13)

Have your actions ever been misunderstood?

WWJD?

And everyone who has left houses or brothers or sisters or father or mother or wife or children or lands, for My name's sake, shall receive a hundredfold, and inherit eternal life.
(Matt. 19:29)

Have you ever worried about what people think of you?

WWJD?

The Spirit Himself bears witness with our spirit that we are children of God. (Rom. 8:16)

Have you ever needed comforting?

WWJD?

These things I have spoken to you, that in Me you may have peace. In the world you will have tribulation; but be of good cheer, I have overcome the world. (John 16:33)

18

W

W

J

D

?

T
H
I
N
K

A
B
O
U
T

I
T

Have you ever grown weary?

WWJD?

There remains therefore a rest for the people of God.
(Heb. 4:9)

Have you ever been lonely?

WWJD?

Indeed the hour is coming, yes, has now come, that you will
be scattered, each to his own, and will leave Me alone. And
yet I am not alone, because the Father is with Me.
(John 16:32)

Have you ever felt useless?

WWJD?

For we are His workmanship, created in Christ Jesus for good works, which God prepared beforehand that we should walk in them. (Eph. 2:10)

Have you ever expected gratitude without receiving it?

WWJD?

For God is not unjust to forget your work and labor of love which you have shown toward His name, in that you have ministered to the saints, and do minister. (Heb. 6:10)

20

W

W

J

D

?

Have you ever been wrongfully accused?

WWJD?

For this is commendable, if because of conscience toward God one endures grief, suffering wrongfully. For what credit is it if, when you are beaten for your faults, you take it patiently? But when you do good and suffer, if you take it patiently, this is commendable before God.
(1 Peter 2:19–20)

Have you ever been afraid to speak out for your faith?

WWJD?

For God has not given us a spirit of fear, but of power and of love and of a sound mind. Therefore do not be ashamed of the testimony of our Lord, nor of me His prisoner, but share with me in the sufferings for the gospel according to the power of God. (2 Tim. 1:7–8)

22

Have you ever been humiliated in public and felt like you could never face anyone again?

WWJD?

Then He took the twelve aside and said to them, "Behold, we are going up to Jerusalem, and all things that are written by the prophets concerning the Son of Man will be accomplished. For He will be delivered to the Gentiles and will be mocked and insulted and spit upon. They will scourge Him and kill Him. And the third day He will rise again." (Luke 18:31–33)

23

Have you ever lacked discipline?

WWJD?

But reject profane and old wives' fables, and exercise yourself toward godliness. For bodily exercise profits a little, but godliness is profitable for all things, having promise of the life that now is and of that which is to come.
(1 Tim. 4:7–8)

24

W

W

J

D

?

Have you ever been embarrassed or shy?

WWJD?

According to my earnest expectation and hope that in nothing I shall be ashamed, but with all boldness, as always, so now also Christ will be magnified in my body, whether by life or by death. (Phil. 1:20)

Have you ever felt unloved?

WWJD?

At that day you will know that I am in My Father, and you in Me, and I in you. He who has My commandments and keeps them, it is he who loves Me. And he who loves Me will be loved by My Father, and I will love him and manifest Myself to him. (John 14:20–21)

26

W

W

J

D

?

PART 3

How Do I Know?
Who Is to Decide?

Rachel Winslow, a member of the First Church choir, is among the volunteers:

"I want to ask a question," said Rachel Winslow. Everyone turned towards her. Her face glowed with a beauty that no physical loveliness could ever create.

"I am a little in doubt as to the source of our knowledge concerning what Jesus would do. Who is to decide for me just what He would do in my case? It is a different age. There are many perplexing questions in our civilization that are not mentioned in the teachings of Jesus. How am I going to tell what He would do?"

"There is no way that I know of," replied the pastor, "except as we study Jesus through the medium of the Holy Spirit. You remember what Christ said speaking to His disciples about the Holy Spirit: 'Howbeit when He the spirit of truth is come. He shall guide you into all the truth; for He shall not speak for Himself; but soever things He shall hear, there shall He speak; and He shall declare unto you the things that are to come. He shall glorify me; for He shall take of mine and declare it unto you. All things whatsoever the Father hath are mine; therefore said I, that He taketh of mine and shall declare it unto you.' There is no other test that I know of. We shall all have to decide what Jesus would do after going to that source of knowledge."

—from Chapter Two of *In His Steps* by Charles Sheldon

Have you ever felt troubled?

WWJD?

But the Helper, the Holy Spirit, whom the Father will send in My name, He will teach you all things, and bring to your remembrance all things that I said to you. Peace I leave with you, My peace I give to you; not as the world gives do I give to you. Let not your heart be troubled, neither let it be afraid. (John 14:26–27)

W

W

J

D

?

THINK ABOUT IT

Have you ever wanted to maintain control of your life?

WWJD?

Then He said to them all, "If anyone desires to come after Me, let him deny himself, and take up his cross daily, and follow Me. For whoever desires to save his life will lose it, but whoever loses his life for My sake will save it. For what profit is it to a man if he gains the whole world, and is himself destroyed or lost?" (Luke 9:23–25)

31

Have you ever felt insecure?

WWJD?

For I am persuaded that neither death nor life, nor angels nor principalities nor powers, nor things present nor things to come, nor height nor depth, nor any other created thing, shall be able to separate us from the love of God which is in Christ Jesus our Lord. (Rom. 8:38–39)

W

W

J

D

?

**T
H
I
N
K

A
B
O
U
T

I
T**

Have you ever doubted yourself?

WWJD?

Being confident of this very thing, that He who has begun a good work in you will complete it until the day of Jesus Christ. (Phil. 1:6)

Have you ever needed guidance?

WWJD?

If any of you lacks wisdom, let him ask of God, who gives to all liberally and without reproach, and it will be given to him. (James 1:5)

Have you ever felt hopeless?

WWJD?

In this you greatly rejoice, though now for a little while, if need be, you have been grieved by various trials, that the genuineness of your faith, being much more precious than gold that perishes, though it is tested by fire, may be found to praise, honor, and glory at the revelation of Jesus Christ. (1 Peter 1:6–7)

34

W

W

J

D

?

Have you ever been somewhere you shouldn't?

WWJD?

*But you, O man of God, flee these things and pursue
righteousness, godliness, faith, love, patience, gentleness.
Fight the good fight of faith, lay hold on eternal life, to
which you were also called and have confessed the good
confession in the presence of many witnesses.
(1 Tim. 6:11–12)*

35

Have you ever doubted God?

WWJD?

Let us hold fast the confession of our hope without wavering, for He who promised is faithful. (Heb. 10:23)

Have you ever been confused?

WWJD?

For where envy and self-seeking exist, confusion and every evil thing are there. But the wisdom that is from above is first pure, then peaceable, gentle, willing to yield, full of mercy and good fruits, without partiality and without hypocrisy. (James 3:16–17)

36

PART 4

Who Shall Oppose Us?

Edward Norman, editor of the Raymond Daily News, *receives opposition from Clark, his managing editor, when Norman decides to omit an account of a prize fight:*

Norman sat silent for a minute. Then he spoke gently but firmly.

"Clark, what in your honest opinion is the right standard for determining conduct? Is the only right standard for every one, the probable action of Jesus Christ? Would you say that the highest, best law for a man to live by was contained in asking the question, 'What would Jesus do?' And then doing it regardless of results? In other words, do you think men everywhere ought to follow Jesus' example as closely as they can in their daily lives?" Clark turned red, and moved uneasily in his chair before he

W

W

J

D

?

answered the editor's question.

"Why—yes—I suppose if you put it on the ground of what men ought to do there is no other standard of conduct. But the question is, What is feasible? Is it possible to make it pay? To succeed in the newspaper business we have got to conform to custom and the recognized methods of society. We can't do as we would in an ideal world."

"Do you mean that we can't run the paper on Christian principles and make it succeed?"

"Yes, that's just what I mean. It can't be done. We'll go bankrupt in thirty days."

Norman did not reply at once. He was very thoughtful.

"We shall have occasion to talk this over again, Clark. Meanwhile I think we ought to understand each other frankly. I have pledged myself for a year to do everything

39

connected with the paper after answering the question, 'What would Jesus do?' as honestly as possible. I shall continue to do this in the belief that not only can we succeed but that we can succeed better than we ever did."
—from Chapter Three of *In His Steps* by Charles Sheldon

W

W

W

J

D

?

Have you ever had your name dragged through the mud?

WWJD?

And the chief priests accused Him of many things, but He answered nothing. Then Pilate asked Him again, saying, "Do You answer nothing? See how many things they testify against You!" But Jesus still answered nothing, so that Pilate marveled. (Mark 15:3–5)

41

Have you ever felt unprotected?

WWJD?

But the Lord is faithful, who will establish you and guard you from the evil one. And we have confidence in the Lord concerning you, both that you do and will do the things we command you. (2 Thess. 3:3–4)

W

W

J

D

?

Have you ever been betrayed by a friend or family member?

WWJD?

Then He said to the disciples, "It is impossible that no offenses should come, but woe to him through whom they do come! It would be better for him if a millstone were hung around his neck, and he were thrown into the sea, than that he should offend one of these little ones. Take heed to yourselves. If your brother sins against you, rebuke him; and if he repents, forgive him. And if he sins against you seven times in a day, and seven times in a day returns to you, saying, 'I repent,' you shall forgive him." (Luke 17:1–4)

Have you ever been cut off in traffic?

WWJD?

So then, my beloved brethren, let every man be swift to hear, slow to speak, slow to wrath; for the wrath of man does not produce the righteousness of God. (James 1:19–20)

Have you ever felt threatened?

WWJD?

What then shall we say to these things? If God is for us, who can be against us? (Rom. 8:31)

W

W

J

D

?

Have you ever been deceived or lied to by a service repairman?

WWJD?

As you therefore have received Christ Jesus the Lord, so walk in Him, rooted and built up in Him and established in the faith, as you have been taught, abounding in it with thanksgiving. Beware lest anyone cheat you through philosophy and empty deceit, according to the tradition of men, according to the basic principles of the world, and not according to Christ. (Col. 2:6–8)

45

Have you ever been taken advantage of?

WWJD?

But I tell you not to resist an evil person. But whoever slaps you on your right cheek, turn the other to him also. If anyone wants to sue you and take away your tunic, let him have your cloak also. And whoever compels you to go one mile, go with him two. Give to him who asks you, and from him who wants to borrow from you do not turn away. (Matt. 5:39–42)

W

W

J

D

?

THINK ABOUT IT

Have you ever been made to feel your best wasn't good enough?

WWJD?

But avoid foolish disputes, genealogies, contentions, and strivings about the law; for they are unprofitable and useless. Reject a divisive man after the first and second admonition, knowing that such a person is warped and sinning, being self-condemned. (Titus 3:9–11)

Have you ever faced heartbreak?

WWJD?

And He said to me, "My grace is sufficient for you, for My strength is made perfect in weakness." Therefore most gladly I will rather boast in my infirmities, that the power of Christ may rest upon me. Therefore I take pleasure in infirmities, in reproaches, in needs, in persecutions, in distresses, for Christ's sake. For when I am weak, then I am strong. (2 Cor. 12:9–10)

48

W

W

J

D

?

PART 5

Priorities of the
Heart

Milton Wright, a merchant in Raymond with over one hundred men employed in his various shops, makes a plan:

"WHAT JESUS WOULD PROBABLY DO
IN MILTON WRIGHT'S PLACE AS A BUSINESS MAN"

1. He would engage in the business first of all for the purpose of glorifying God, and not for the primary purpose of making money.
2. All money that might be made he would never regard as his own, but as trust funds to be used for the good of humanity.
3. His relations with all the persons in his employ would be the most loving and helpful. He could not help thinking of all of them in the light of souls to be saved. This

50

W

W

J

D

?

thought would always be greater than his thought of making money in the business.

4. He would never do a single dishonest or questionable thing or try in any remotest way to get the advantage of any one else in the same business.

5. The principle of unselfishness and helpfulness in the business would direct all its details.

6. Upon this principle he would shape the entire plan of his relations to his employees, to the people who were his customers and to the general business world with which he was connected.

    —from Chapter Nine of *In His Steps* by Charles Sheldon

Have you ever made excuses?

WWJD?

This I say, therefore, and testify in the Lord, that you should no longer walk as the rest of the Gentiles walk, in the futility of their mind, having their understanding darkened, being alienated from the life of God, because of the ignorance that is in them, because of the blindness of their heart. (Eph. 4:17–18)

52

W

W

J

D

?

Have you ever said no when you *knew* you should say yes?

WWJD?

And whatever you do, do it heartily, as to the Lord and not to men, knowing that from the Lord you will receive the reward of the inheritance; for you serve the Lord Christ. But he who does wrong will be repaid for what he has done, and there is no partiality. (Col. 3:23–25)

53

Have you ever just slept in to avoid work, school, church?

WWJD?

And we desire that each one of you show the same diligence to the full assurance of hope until the end, that you do not become sluggish, but imitate those who through faith and patience inherit the promises. (Heb. 6:11–12)

54

W

W

J

D

?

T
H
I
N
K

A
B
O
U
T

I
T

Have you ever tried to avoid people who are not like you?

WWJD?

And those members of the body which we think to be less honorable, on these we bestow greater honor; and our unpresentable parts have greater modesty, but our presentable parts have no need. But God composed the body, having given greater honor to that part which lacks it, that there should be no schism in the body, but that the members should have the same care for one another.
(1 Cor. 12:23–25)

Have you ever had to fire someone?

WWJD?

Now no chastening seems to be joyful for the present, but painful; nevertheless, afterward it yields the peaceable fruit of righteousness to those who have been trained by it. Therefore strengthen the hands which hang down, and the feeble knees, and make straight paths for your feet, so what is lame may not be dislocated, but rather be healed. (Heb. 12:11–13)

W

W

J

D

?

Have you ever been asked to violate your moral values?

WWJD?

Be sober, be vigilant; because your adversary the devil walks about like a roaring lion, seeking whom he may devour. Resist him, steadfast in the faith, knowing that the same sufferings are experienced by your brotherhood in the world. (1 Peter 5:8–9)

Have you ever been a worrywart?

WWJD?

Therefore I say to you, do not worry about your life, what you will eat or what you will drink; nor about your body, what you will put on. Is not life more than food and the body more than clothing? . . . Which of you by worrying can add one more cubit to his stature? (Matt. 6:25, 27)

W

W

J

D

?

Have you ever wanted to start over and couldn't?

WWJD?

Brethren, I do not count myself to have apprehended; but one thing I do, forgetting those things which are behind and reaching forward to those things which are ahead, I press toward the goal for the prize of the upward call of God in Christ Jesus. (Phil. 3:13–14)

Have you ever faced financial ruin?

WWJD?

Now godliness with contentment is great gain. For we brought nothing into this world, and it is certain we can carry nothing out. And having food and clothing, with these we shall be content. (1 Tim. 6:6–8)

W

W

J

D

?

PART 6

Narrow Is the Gate

Donald Marsh, president of Lincoln College is challenged to use his sphere of influence in the community:

"Yet all these years I, with nearly every teacher in the college, have been satisfied to let other men run the municipality and have lived in a little world of my own, out of touch and sympathy with the real world of people. 'What would Jesus do?' I have even tried to avoid an honest answer. I can no longer do so. My plain duty is to take a personal part in this coming election, go to the primaries, throw the weight of my influence, whatever it is, toward the nomination and election of good men, and plunge into the very depths of the entire horrible whirlpool of deceit, bribery, political trickery and saloonism as it exists in Raymond today. I would sooner walk up to the mouth of a cannon any time than do this. I

W

W

J

D

?

dread it because I hate the touch of the whole matter. I would give almost any thing to be able to say, 'I do not believe Jesus would do anything of the sort.' But I am more and more persuaded that He would. This is where the suffering comes for me. It would hurt me half so much to lose my position or my home. I loathe the contact with this municipal problem. I would so much prefer to remain quietly in my scholastic life with classes in Ethics and Philosophy. But the call has come to me so plainly that I cannot escape. 'Donald Marsh, follow me. Do your duty as a citizen of Raymond at the point where your citizenship will cost you something. Help to cleanse this municipal stable, even if you have to soil your aristocratic feelings a little.' Maxwell, this is my cross, I must take it up or deny my Lord."

—from Chapter Eleven of *In His Steps* by Charles Sheldon **63**

Have you ever been called to serve on a jury?

WWJD?

Therefore submit yourselves to every ordinance of man for the Lord's sake, whether to the king as supreme, or to governors, as to those who are sent by him for the punishment of evildoers and for the praise of those who do good. (1 Peter 2:13–14)

64

W

W

J

D

?

Have you ever failed to do the right thing?

WWJD?

*But I have prayed for you, that your faith should not fail;
and when you have returned to Me, strengthen your
brethren. (Luke 22:32)*

Have you ever been rebellious?

WWJD?

*Beware, brethren, lest there be in any of you an evil heart
of unbelief in departing from the living God; but exhort one
another daily, while it is called "Today," lest any of you be
hardened through the deceitfulness of sin. (Heb. 3:12–13)*

Have you ever driven over the speed limit or run a stop sign?

WWJD?

Let every soul be subject to the governing authorities. For there is no authority except from God, and the authorities that exist are appointed by God. Therefore whoever resists the authority resists the ordinance of God, and those who resist will bring judgment on themselves. (Rom. 13:1–2)

66

W

W

J

D

?

Have you ever received too much change?

WWJD?

*He who is faithful in what is least is faithful also in much;
and he who is unjust in what is least is unjust also in much.
Therefore if you have not been faithful in the unrighteous
mammon, who will commit to your trust the true riches?
And if you have not been faithful in what is another man's,
who will give you what is your own? (Luke 16:10–12)*

67

Have you ever gossiped?

WWJD?

But I say to you that for every idle word men may speak, they will give account of it in the day of judgment. For by your words you will be justified, and by your words you will be condemned. (Matt. 12:36–37)

W

W

J

D

?

Have you ever been to a movie you should have walked out on or watched a TV show you shouldn't have?

WWJD?

Finally, brethren, whatever things are true, whatever things are noble, whatever things are just, whatever things are pure, whatever things are lovely, whatever things are of good report, if there is any virtue and if there is anything praiseworthy—meditate on these things. (Phil. 4:8)

Have you ever failed a test?

WWJD?

While we do not look at the things which are seen, but at the things which are not seen. For the things which are seen are temporary, but the things which are not seen are eternal. (2 Cor. 4:18)

70

Have you ever wanted to take revenge?

WWJD?

For we know Him who said, "Vengeance is Mine, I will repay," says the Lord. And again, "The LORD will judge His people." (Heb. 10:30)

Have you ever won first place?

WWJD?

But "he who glories, let him glory in the LORD." For not he who commends himself is approved, but whom the Lord commends. (2 Cor. 10:17–18)

71

PART 7

"Go and Do
Likewise . . ."

Miss Virginia Page, heiress:

Finally a thought possessed her that she could not escape. What was to hinder her from taking Loreen home with her? Why should not this homeless, wretched creature, reeking with the fumes of liquor, be cared for in Virginia's own home instead of being consigned to strangers in some hospital or house of charity? Virginia really knew very little about any such places of refuge. As a matter of fact, there were two or three such institutions in Raymond, but it is doubtful if any of them would have taken a person like Loreen in her present condition. But that was not the question with Virginia just now. "What would Jesus do with Loreen?" That was what Virginia

faced, and she finally answered it by touching the girl
again.

"Loreen, come. You are going home with me."

—from Chapter Twelve of *In His Steps* by Charles Sheldon

Have you ever had a dispute with a neighbor?

WWJD?

He who would love life
And see good days,
Let him refrain his tongue from evil,
And his lips from speaking deceit.
Let him turn away from evil and do good;
Let him seek peace and pursue it. (1 Peter 3:10–11)

W

W

J

D

?

Have you ever lacked compassion?

WWJD?

"So which of these three do you think was neighbor to him who fell among the thieves?" And he said, "He who showed mercy on him." Then Jesus said to him, "Go and do likewise." (Luke 10:36–37)

Have you ever disappointed your friends?

WWJD?

Let nothing be done through selfish ambition or conceit, but in lowliness of mind let each esteem others better than himself. Let each of you look out not only for his own interests, but also for the interests of others. (Phil. 2:3–4)

W

W

J

D

?

78

Have you ever been asked to give more than you could afford?

WWJD?

Now Jesus sat opposite the treasury and saw how the people put money into the treasury. And many who were rich put in much. Then one poor widow came and threw in two mites, which make a quadrans. So He called His disciples to Himself and said to them, "Assuredly, I say to you that this poor widow has put in more than all those who have given to the treasury; for they all put in out of their abundance, but she out of her poverty put in all that she had, her whole livelihood." (Mark 12:41–44)

79

Have you ever needed to give comfort?

WWJD?

Blessed be the God and Father of our Lord Jesus Christ, the Father of mercies and God of all comfort, who comforts us in all our tribulation, that we may be able to comfort those who are in any trouble, with the comfort with which we ourselves are comforted by God. (2 Cor. 1:3–5)

W

W

J

D

?

80

THINK ABOUT IT

Have you ever made an unwise choice of friends?

WWJD?

Do not be deceived: "Evil company corrupts good habits." Awake to righteousness and do not sin; for some do not have the knowledge of God. (1 Cor. 15:33–34b)

Have you ever disappointed your parents or your children?

WWJD?

Now I rejoice, not that you were made sorry, but that your sorrow led to repentance. For you were made sorry in a godly manner, that you might suffer loss from us in nothing. (2 Cor. 7:9)

81

Have you ever been a busybody?

WWJD?

For we hear that there are some who walk among you in a disorderly manner, not working at all, but are busybodies. Now those who are such we command and exhort through our Lord Jesus Christ that they work in quietness and eat their own bread. (2 Thess. 3:11–12)

W

W

J

D

?

Has your body ever been wracked with pain?

WWJD?

Therefore we do not lose heart. Even though our outward man is perishing, yet the inward man is being renewed day by day. For our light affliction, which is but for a moment, is working for us a far more exceeding and eternal weight of glory, while we do not look at the things which are seen, but at the things which are not seen. For the things which are seen are temporary, but the things which are not seen are eternal. (2 Cor. 4:16–18)

83

ABOUT THE AUTHOR

Beverly Courrege is co-owner of Courrege Design, a Christian gift manufacturer, and author of the bestseller *WWJD: Answers to What Would Jesus Do?* Her other books include the *WWJD Journal* and *WWJD? The Question That Will Change Your Life* with Paul Meier, M.D., and Heidi Gardiner. She and her husband live in Dallas, Texas.

W

W

J

D

?